Tracing Our
JAPANESE
Roots

GARY KAWAGUCHI

John Muir Publications
Santa Fe, New Mexico

Acknowledgments
Special thanks to consultant Dr. Lane Hirabayashi of the Center for Studies of Race and Ethnicity, University of Colorado, Boulder. Thanks also to Ming Xin Kawaguchi for his help in editing.

This book is dedicated to my parents

First edition.   First printing January 1995
First TWG printing January 1995

Library of Congress Cataloging-in-Publication Data
Kawaguchi, Gary. 1954
American origins : tracing our Japanese roots / by Gary Kawaguchi.
  p. cm.
  Includes index.
  ISBN 1-56261-159-3 : $12.95
1. Japanese Americans—History—Juvenile literature. [1. Japanese Americans—History.
2. United States—Emigration and immigration.] I. Title
E184.J3S24 1994
973.04956—dc20

93-48125
CIP
AC 94

Editorial: Elizabeth Wolf, Julie Lefevre
Production: Kathryn Lloyd-Strongin, Chris Brigman
Logo design: Peter Aschwanden
Interior design: Ken Wilson
Illustrations: David Aragon
Typesetting: Linda Braun
Printer: Arcata Graphics/Kingsport

Distributed to the book trade by
W. W. Norton & Co., Inc.
500 Fifth Avenue
New York, New York 10110

Distributed to the education market by
Wright Group Publishing, Inc.
19201 120th Avenue N.E.
Bothell, WA 98011-9512

Cover photo: Boy at the wheel of a tractor, San Francisco, 1928. UPI/Bettmann
Title page photo: Los Angeles County family subject to evacuation orders, 1942. Underwood Photo
    Archives, San Francisco
Contents page photo: Japanese Children arriving in California, 1920. UPI/Bettmann
Back cover photo: Jim's Cafe, Pioneer Square, Seattle, ca.1940. Photo courtesy Aki Kurose/The Wing
    Luke Asian Museum

CONTENTS

THE ADVENTURE BEGINS

Japan is a cluster of islands off the coasts of Korea and China, in the North Pacific Ocean. For hundreds of years Japan had very little contact with other countries. But in the mid-1800s, Commodore Matthew Perry, a U.S. Navy admiral, sailed into a Japanese harbor with a fleet of American gunships. Japan realized that it could not protect itself from other countries' military power. The Japanese government agreed to trade with the United States and started to build a new, modern country.

Peasants were charged extra taxes to pay the costs of building a powerful army and navy and starting new industries. Many farmers had to sell their land to pay the taxes. In the late 1800s, thousands of Japanese left their homeland to work in the Hawaiian Islands and the United States. They wanted to save money and return to Japan rich.

Plantation owners in Hawaii promised good pay and working conditions for those who came to work in their pineapple and sugarcane fields. Many Japanese left their families and their culture to work long hours for low pay. These Japanese people were immigrating—they were leaving their homeland to live and work in another country.

This ship in Yokahama, Japan, carried immigrants to the United States

How Many Japanese Came to the United States?

The Continental U.S.:

Decade	Number
1861-1870	218
1871-1880	149
1881-1890	2,270
1891-1900	27,982
1901-1907	108,163
1908-1914	74,478
1915-1924	85,197
1925-1940	6,156

Hawaii:

Year	Number
1868	148
1885-1898	45,034
1899	19,908

In all, nearly 370,000 Japanese immigrated to the United States and Hawaii. Today, about 850,000 people of Japanese descent live in the U.S.

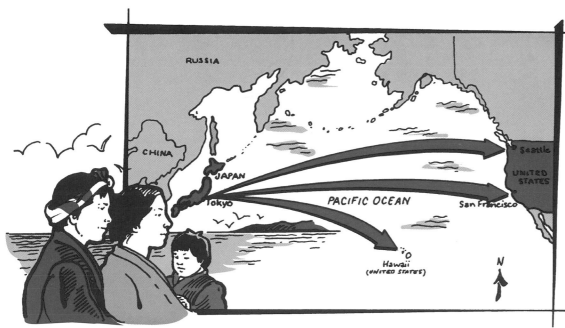

Early Japanese immigrants settled in Hawaii and on the West Coast of the mainland

In the United States, the West Coast was growing in population and needed workers. Chinese workers had been recruited from China to do many kinds of hard labor, including building America's first transcontinental railroad. But beginning in 1882, they were excluded from the United States. After that date, Japanese workers were used to replace Chinese workers.

But by the time the Japanese immigrants came, they were not welcomed by most people in the United States. They were not allowed to become citizens, own land, live wherever they wished, or work in many types of employment. After the United States went to war with Japan during World War II, Japanese families were forced to leave their homes and move to internment camps. The government made them stay in the camps—which were like prisons—just because they were of Japanese descent. It was a shameful chapter in United States history.

The Japanese immigrant pioneers and their children had to overcome problems of language and cultural differences, racist laws, and neighbors who hated them because they were Japanese. But they succeeded. Many started farms and businesses of their own. Japanese American farmers helped make California one of the biggest suppliers of fresh green vegetables in the country.

Even though many people did not want Japanese immigrants to be in the United States, the Japanese endured and were always proud of their heritage. Their children and grandchildren became successful Americans. Many of them went to college, and some are now well known across the country.

This is the story of Japanese Americans from the immigrant generation to the present. It is only one part of the story of America, and another reason why life in America is so rich in culture.

A Japanese American family

3

MEIJI ERA JAPAN

For hundreds of years Japan was ruled by the leaders of the *samurai* (sah-moo-rye), or warrior class. The most powerful *samurai* were called *daimyo* (die-myoh) They controlled land and vassals, men who were loyal to them. The most powerful of all was the *shogun* (shoh-goon). The *shogun* was the ruler of all the *daimyo*, and the head of the *Bakufu* (bahk-foo), the military government that ran the country. The emperor had very little power.

It was a time very much like medieval Europe (A.D. 900–1200). *Daimyo* were like kings who controlled most of the land in Japan. The *samurai* were like the knights in Europe, the people in society who could wear swords and wage war. The *daimyo* and

Officials of the Meiji government, 1889

A *traditional warrior of old Japan*

A small group of *Bakufu* supporters left Japan in 1869 and started a farming community in Northern California. It was named the Wakamatsu Colony, after the Japanese prefecture (something like a state) they came from. It was also called the Gold Hill colony, after a nearby town. The immigrants tried to grow silk for fabric, but their project failed. Most of them returned to Japan. The colony is best remembered for a teen-aged girl named Okei, who is believed to be the first Japanese woman to die in the United States. She was buried near the colony.

Commodore Perry arrived in Japan in 1853

samurai made money by collecting taxes from peasants. The peasants, though, were often taxed more than they could afford and lived in poverty, close to starvation.

The *Bakufu* allowed only limited contact with the outside world for more than two hundred years. They even made it illegal for Japanese to leave the country.

But in 1853, when Commodore Perry sailed into Edo Bay, Japan's government and culture were forced to change. The Japanese navy could not defend the country against the modern American steam-powered battleships. So the *Bakufu* had no choice but to allow trade with the United States, and later with European countries.

Japanese leaders argued about the future, but finally agreed that their country would have to learn new technologies and build a modern military, especially a navy. There was a brief revolution called the Meiji Restoration in 1868. It was called a restoration because the young Emperor Meiji, who was only 15 years old, was restored as the head of government. Most of the supporters of the Bakufu were killed.

During the Meiji Era, Japan went from being an isolated nation to being a world power in a very short time. The Meiji Era (1867–1912) was a time of great change. For the first time in hundreds of years, Japan looked outside of its islands for new ideas. Travel and study in Europe and the United States were allowed.

The new government made *samurai*, including the *daimyo*, common citizens. Many *daimyo* lost their land, and the government was run by people who were not of royal birth or from high-ranking families. Travel overseas became legal, with the aim of sending Japanese to gather knowledge useful to the country. The Japanese military became strong enough during Emperor Meiji's reign to defeat China and Russia. It was a quick rise to power for a country that only a few decades before had never seen steamships.

FAMILY LIFE

In a Japanese household, all generations lived together. The Japanese word *ie* (ee-eh) means more than just a family with a father, mother, and their children. It often includes the grandfather and grandmother, sometimes uncles and aunts, more distant relatives, and even people who were unrelated. They could all be considered as family. An *ie* could also include more than one household.

The overall head of the household was usually the grandfather. It could also be the oldest son, called the *chonan* (choh-non), if he were married and had children. The grandmother was usually the head of the domestic side of the household. The daughter-in-law would take care of her children and her parents-in-law. The land and house were passed down from the father to

Japanese women and children catch fish for the family meal

the oldest son. During the feudal period, most farming couples decided to marry on their own. Parents were asked for their consent. Sometimes, if there were only daughters in the family, a son-in-law would take on the family name and fill the role of the *chonan*.

The time of year most important to any Japanese household has always been New Year's, or *Oshogatsu* (oh-shoh-gah-tsoo). During the Meiji Era, *Oshogatsu* began to be celebrated the first week of January on the Gregorian calendar, which is the calendar used in Europe and North America. It was the time of year when debts were paid off and special food was prepared. Many New Year's foods became favorites all year long. One of these is *mochi* (moh-chee), a tasty cake made by pounding a special kind of rice to a sticky consistency.

A *traditional outdoor kitchen in Japan, around* 1890

Meals were served at a low table on the floor in Japanese homes

Later, during the Meiji Era, it became more common for the head of the household to decide who the adult children were going to marry. That type of marriage is usually referred to as an arranged marriage. Arranged marriages were always common with *daimyo* and higher *samurai*, but during the Meiji Era, they became popular among the lower classes, too.

The typical farm household had four to six rooms. The floors of a Japanese house were covered with *tatami* (tah-tah-mee), a floor covering filled with straw and tied into mats. Living space doubled as sleeping space at night, when thick blankets called *futon* (foo-tone) were laid down on the *tatami*. The home life centered around the hearth, used for heat and cooking. A hook to hold a pot hung over the fire pit and smoke escaped through a hole in the ceiling. At meal time, the family members would gather around the fire and eat together.

Food for many rural families was very modest. White rice was and still is the main staple (food eaten for most meals) of Japan. Many families, however, could only afford to eat wheat, barley, or millet most of the time. The poorest families could eat only the rice bran, the brown outer coating that is taken off the rice grain. They made pickled vegetables, called *sukemono* (soo-keh-moh-noh), to eat with the rice. Soy beans were prepared in many different ways. Hot green tea, or *ocha* (oh-chah), was the most popular Japanese beverage for rich and poor. Fish was eaten more often than meat because Japan is surrounded by water and there is little land on which animals can be raised.

Children play a game of hopscotch

WORK

Most of the Japanese who immigrated to the United States were farmers and fishing people. Many of them came from the southern part of the largest island, Honshu, and the southern island, Kyushu. Life in Japan in the 1800s and early 1900s was hard for most farmers.

To survive, all the farmers or fishermen in a village had to work together. Many farming or fishing techniques required cooperation. The unwritten rule was that if one or more families needed help, all the others would pitch in. One never knew when one's own family would need help.

The oldest son almost always did the same type of work as his father. He was expected to carry on the work of the father and care for his parents in their old age.

Younger sons did not usually inherit land, so when they married and left home, they had to find jobs or buy their own farm land. Each family had many children so that there would be enough boys to work, and the parents would have someone to care for them when they grew old.

Boys were considered more valuable to

Women feeding silk worms

To make extra money, many households grew silk worms. Silk was a popular material for cloth which was in demand all over the world. Peasant women were in charge of growing the worms. The worms were fed mulberry leaves, which the women grew themselves. The worms would eat night and day and had to be kept warm and dry. Finally, the worms would stop eating and wrap themselves in thin threads of silk to form cocoons. The cocoons were usually sold to cloth manufacturers, who would unravel the silk to make thread to be woven into clothes.

The Japanese harvested mulberry leaves as food for silk worms

All the villagers worked together to plant rice

the farming family because they did the farm labor. In hard times, many young girls and boys were sent to live with families in cities. Girls took care of the family's younger children and did housework. Boys worked as apprentices—low-paid trainees who learned a trade and could later start their own business.

Life in rural Japan revolved around the growing seasons of the most important crop—rice. Villagers had to cooperate in planting, irrigating (bringing water to the fields), and harvesting the grain. Rice was used like money in the feudal period, to pay for taxes.

For many years, villagers in Japan had grown or made all the food, clothes, and housing that they needed for daily life. There was not much need for money. But this began to change during the Meiji Era.

More and more, farmers had to work harder to make ends meet. They grew silk worms and cotton to sell for cash so they could pay their taxes. Sometimes, for the family to survive, one or more family members, usually a teenage son or a daughter, would have to go away to work. These workers were called *dekasegi* (deh-kah-seh-gee). *Dekasegi* usually went to another village or town to a factory where many workers lived together. They were made to work long hours, often under dangerous conditions, for very little money. Many were injured or became sick and died.

The *dekasegi* tradition was well established by the middle of the Meiji Era. Because families were already sending members away to work, it was just another step to send them to the Hawaiian Islands (which weren't yet a part of the U.S.) and America, where wages were much higher.

Fishermen on Japan's Inland Sea, around 1890

EDUCATION

Though life was hard for parents and children alike at times, children were very much loved and valued. The Japanese are known for being very strict and orderly, but until the age of seven, Japanese children received almost no correction or instruction from their parents! Japanese children grew up very close to their mothers, who carried them everywhere with them and would sleep with them at night. Children could fall asleep whenever they wanted to and were almost never left alone.

After the age of seven, however, children had to work. They learned by example, not by words. First the parents and then the other villagers taught them to be dependent on others and to work well in groups, which prepared them for life in the family and the village.

Fathers and mothers could teach their children how to do farming and house work. But in the new Japan, different types of workers were needed. The Meiji government realized that education was the way to build a new, modern country.

Very young children were carried by their mothers at all times

These Japanese children are studying calligraphy

You think *you* have a hard time learning how to spell words! Japanese children have to learn two phonetic alphabets, and pictographs. Phonetic alphabets contain letters that stand for spoken sounds. Pictographs are picture-based characters. *Hiragana* (hee-rah-gah-nah) and *Katakana* (kah-tah-kah-nah) are the phonetic methods of writing. *Kanji* (kahn-jee) are Japanese picture-based characters that were originally borrowed from the Chinese language. To be a literate person in Japan, one has to know thousands of *kanji*.

Universal education, or education for all, became the policy of the land. Both boys and girls were educated and literacy (reading and writing skills) was quickly raised. By the early 1900s, 90 percent of school-age children were attending schools. Today, Japan has one of the highest literacy rates in the world.

Education was not only for teaching reading, writing, and mathematics. It also included training on what was right and wrong, and on good habits to make the Japanese child into a good worker. One important role of the school system was to teach children an unquestioning belief in their country. Among other things, they were taught that the emperor was descended from the gods that created the Japanese people.

The new education rules made sure that everyone had the same instruction for the first six years. In grammar school, everyone learned the same things, no matter what their background. After grammar school, girls and boys went to different schools. Girls were taught skills which would help them be good wives and mothers. Boys went to job training schools which prepared them for life as wage earners.

Some students who were wealthy or smart enough continued their studies at schools that prepared them for college. For most farming families, college was not possible for their children. Colleges were only in the large cities and were very expensive. Few boys were able to go to college, and almost no girls.

The Meiji government sent all children to school. This is a classroom in the 1890s.

THE LIFE OF WOMEN

From birth to death, Japanese women lived very differently than men. Most girls and women had little control over their lives.

All children were supposed to attend at least six years of school, but many girls were unable to. The young girls who did attend school often had to take care of their younger brothers or sisters while in class. If the baby cried, they would have to leave the room. Those girls who had been sent away from home to work for other families were not able to attend school at all.

A girl born in Japan could hope only to be a wife and mother, and look forward to a life of hard work. Survival was very difficult for a woman on her own.

Most people in Japan made their living by farming or fishing. A farmer's wife led a hard life. She rarely left the house, farm, and family. She had to obey her husband, father-in-law, and most of all, her mother-in-law.

Husbands often divorced their wives if they did not meet the family standards. The mother-in-law taught the new bride how to do the household chores. Wives often lived in fear of the mother-in-law. If the mother-in-law did not like the wife's

A *peasant woman washing lettuce with her baby on her back*

Library of Congress

behavior or attitude, she would yell at her and treat her harshly. If the wife did not have any children, she would be sent back to her parents. Most farming families had many children, which made the mother's job more difficult.

The wife was the first one up and last one to sleep. She would be the one to start the fire for cooking and to warm the house.

Peabody Essex Museum, Salem, Mass.

Japanese girls did the family sewing

Girls in Japan have a special holiday. It is called *hina matsuri* (hee-nah maht-soo-ree), or the doll's festival. The custom is over 300 years old. On March 3, dolls dressed in royal costumes are displayed on shelves. Girls have parties, sharing food and drink and offering them to the dolls. The dolls are very expensive and elaborate. They are handed down from generation to generation.

She would be the last to eat at meal times. She would keep the fire going for the *ofuro* (oh-foo-roh), or bath, at night. Everyone in the household would bathe before her. When everyone else had gone to bed, she could finally rest. She worked every waking moment—and hardly had enough time to eat!

Farming wives also worked in the fields. They usually planted the rice seedlings and shared in the harvesting work. If they were married to store owners, they did a lot of the everyday work in the store. Fishing villages and mountain logging communities began to do some farming or silk worm growing to make ends meet. Women would do all the farming or silk worm growing in those communities.

There were some villages in Japan where the women did the fishing by diving under water. Women were also responsible for selling the fish in most fishing villages. In most households all over the country, Japanese wives typically managed the money.

Women who were not married had few options. Poor women worked in textile factories and as maids for rich families. Some women became Buddhist nuns. They were

Mothers and daughters worked hard doing the family wash

much like Catholic nuns. They never married and lived their lives dedicated to the Buddhist faith.

Taking a bath in a wooden tub, around 1880

13

RELIGION IN EVERYDAY LIFE

The only time that everyone could take a well-earned break from work was during festivals, called *matsuri* (maht-soo-ree). In Japan, religion, art and everyday life were all practiced together. *Matsuri* were and still are a popular way for Japanese people to practice their religion. Combining music, dance, and other arts, Japanese people, and especially children, could have fun and celebrate their lives.

Matsuri were almost always linked with the seasonal life of the farmer, especially rice growing. They were like vacations, but with a purpose. *Matsuri* marked plowing, planting, and harvesting times. During those times, farmers could give their thanks to the gods and pray for a good harvest after the next season.

Each farmer's celebration might be different from his neighbor's. In Japan, people often followed the religious beliefs and practices of many different religions. These religions were often mixed together to form a unique way of worshipping.

Shinto, the oldest and most Japanese religion, celebrated many gods in everyday life. In Shinto belief, plants, animals, and food all have spirits. The farmer believed that Shinto protected his harvests, the fisherman believed it protected his catch.

Shinto festivals also revered the spirits of ancestors. The dead were thought to watch over and protect the living. People were considered to be pure and good, and

Exciting ghost stories were told during Obon, *the Buddhist harvest Festival*

A favorite activity during *Obon* is telling ghost stories. People all over the world enjoy listening to chilling tales in the dark. Long ago, people in Japan believed in ghosts, magical talking animals and demons. During *Obon*, it was a joyful activity to welcome the spirits of relatives back to their homes. However, it was believed that people who had died violent or painful deaths, or had been troubled while alive, could return to bother the living.

During the Shinto harvest ceremony people prayed for good crops

bad acts were the result of evil spirits. The evil could be expelled from a person by performing prayers and making offerings to the gods.

The New Year celebration, *Oshogatsu*, (oh-shoh-gaht-soo) was very much a Shinto event. Purifying oneself and one's household was done to keep evil away. Offerings and prayers were made to all the gods to make the coming year prosperous.

Buddhism is another religion that was important to Japanese festivals. Buddhism started in India and was brought to Japan by Chinese and Korean monks. It taught the importance of living a good life. Buddhists believe in reincarnation, which means that a person can be reborn into other lives with the goal of improving one's soul.

Obon (oh-bone), a celebration which comes around harvest time, in the late summer or early fall, was the second most important *matsuri* in Japan. *Obon* was the time when Buddhists believed that souls of the dead returned to the homes in which they had lived. Food was offered to them. Dancing, or *odori* (oh-doh-ree), was also

an important part of the celebration.

The philosophy of *bushido* (boo-shee-doh) is just as important as the religions. It is the code of the *samurai*, in which honor and loyalty are foremost. The celebration known as Boy's Day was a day devoted to the warrior spirit. Now it is known as Children's Day, and is not devoted solely to boys or to the warrior's code. *Bushido* still lives on in the Japanese way of life.

Children celebrate Boy's Day, around 1890

FAMOUS PEOPLE OF THE MEIJI ERA

Ryoma Sakamoto (1835–1867)

Ryoma Sakamoto was a low-ranking *samurai* from Tosa prefecture. He had little education, but rose quickly as a leader because of his intelligence. He was in Edo when Commodore Perry sailed in with his gunships. He helped start a naval military school that was organized by the Bakufu government. He later believed that the Bakufu government was not able to modernize Japan and worked to change the government.

Sakamoto worked out an agreement between the Choshu and Satsuma prefectures. The two prefectures were well known for having the strongest armies. With their combined forces, the Bakufu government was overturned.

Sakamoto believed that Japan's government should become a democracy, a system where the citizens have supreme power. He wanted to get rid of the feudal system, where a few men controlled most of the land and the government. But Sakamoto never saw the change in government. He was assassinated—killed by someone who didn't like his political beliefs—in 1867.

Toshimichi Okubo (1831–1878)

Toshimichi Okubo became the most powerful government official in the early Meiji period. He performed the role of a prime minister, an office much like a president, though no such position existed at the time.

A native of Satsuma prefecture, Okubo was one of the leaders of the Restoration. He headed the Meiji government until he was assassinated in 1878.

Many of Okubo's reforms are still the basis of Japanese government policies to this day. Okubo believed that the government could improve the economy by helping businesses.

Okubo saw the need to develop all of Japan's resources. Japan had and still has to support many people with little good farming land. Using Okubo's ideas, the Meiji government encouraged some farmers to move to the northern island of Hokkaido. Okubo wanted all of the islands

Ryoma Sakamoto started a naval academy

Yukichi Fukuzawa believed in educating all children, rich or poor

of Japan to be developed so that the resources would be used to build up the country. In ten short years, he started Japan on the path to modernity.

Yukichi Fukuzawa (1835–1901)

Yukichi Fukuzawa was a powerful leader in the early Meiji Era. He helped change the Japanese education system. Fukuzawa believed that everyone should be educated, whether they were rich or poor. He wanted all children to get a good education, so everyone had the chance to succeed.

Fukuzawa also worked for women's rights in education and in every aspect of life. He was not able to see his ideas of women's rights put into action, but thanks to him, many more women had a formal education. He also believed in children learning science and other practical studies. Fukuzawa developed his ideas after studying Dutch and English, reading widely, and visiting the United States.

Motoko Hani (1873-1957)

Motoko Hani was the first woman journalist in Japanese history. She was born the year after the Meiji government opened its first public schools. She was in the first graduating class of Tokyo First Higher Women's School, a pioneering secondary school for women. One of the first women to graduate from college in Japan, Hani began her journalism career at the *Hochi* newspaper. The fact that she was hired was remarkable in itself. At the time, few women worked anywhere outside of the home. Modern journalism had begun only a few decades before she entered the profession.

Hani became known for her stories about social problems and the lives of ordinary people, especially women. She started a women's magazine called *Fujin no Tomo*, or "Women's Friend," which is the oldest women's publication in Japan.

Motoko Hani interviewed people about their lives for her newspaper stories

THE VOYAGE TO AMERICA

Very few of the first Japanese immigrants to the United States had been outside of Japan before or knew anyone who had. They were mostly young men and a few young women. Many were still in their teens.

There were many confusing changes that met the traveler who left Japan for the first time. The trip was made by steamship across the Pacific Ocean, and it took many weeks. It was crowded on board, with many people thrown together in close quarters. Add to this that many people were seasick, and the journey was quite unpleasant. It was long and boring, with unfamiliar food that did not taste good to them.

Perhaps the most difficult thing for the new immigrants was leaving their families behind in Japan. The Japanese family was very close, especially children and their parents. It was thought that a good son would sacrifice anything for his parents. Some immigrants left hoping to make enough money to help their parents meet debts or buy back their family land. Of course, some of the immigrants mainly wanted to find some adventure or avoid being drafted into the army.

For the young Japanese men and women who made up most of the early Japanese immigration to America, the new country offered a chance for a better life. It also offered a way to break free from Japan's strict social structure. In Japan, if you were born into a farming or fishing family, it was

Hikozo Hamada, the first Japanese American citizen, met President Lincoln

The first Japanese person to become a United States citizen arrived in America by accident. In 1851, when he was only 13 years old, Hikozo Hamada was a sailor on a Japanese boat that was stranded at sea for 50 days. The crew was rescued by an American ship and taken to the United States. Hikozo Hamada decided to stay on in the new country. He became a citizen and was even introduced to President Abraham Lincoln. After that he changed his name to Joseph Heco.

On a steamship bound for San Francisco, 1920

and is given to the first generation living in a country outside of Japan. The *Issei* that came to the United States were also the first large group to leave Japan. Before then it was illegal to leave their homeland.

Japanese later moved all over the world. When Japanese were no longer allowed to go to the United States, many went to Brazil and other parts of South America. Many more went to live in Northern China until the end of World War II.

Between 1890 and 1920, about 300,000 adventurous Japanese journeyed across the Pacific Ocean to Hawaii and California. Many of them did not stay more than a few years. But some remained and started families. This is very surprising when one considers that it was impossible for *Issei* to become U.S. citizens until 1952, with the passage of the MacCarran-Walter Act. Japanese laborers were restricted from coming to the United States beginning in 1907, and almost no immigrants were allowed into the U.S. after 1924. Even so, from 1910 to 1970 the Japanese were the largest Asian ethnic group in the United States.

difficult to become anything other than a fisherman or a farmer. But after arriving and working for other people in America, many Japanese were able to start their own farms and businesses. That would have been very difficult in Japan.

The first generation of Japanese to immigrate to America were called *Issei* (ee-say). The name means "first generation"

Immigrant children arrive in California, 1920

THE FIRST DESTINATION: HAWAII

For Japanese immigrants, from 1880 to 1890, Hawaii was the main destination. Hawaii is a group of islands in the Pacific Ocean about halfway between Japan and the United States. At that time, Hawaii was an independent country ruled by a king.

Hawaiian plantations were able to sell their sugar freely to the United States. The plantations were becoming larger, and there were not enough workers in Hawaii. Workers had been brought from China to work for a few years under contract. But as soon as the contracts were completed, the Chinese workers did not want to work on the plantations any longer. Japanese workers replaced them.

Many *Issei* workers landed in Hawaii because of a treaty with Japan to import laborers. The agreement was arranged by Robert Walker Irwin, who worked for the Hawaii plantation owners. Irwin was friends with the Japanese foreign minister, Inoue Kaoru, and Masuda Takashi, an importer, both from Choshu prefecture. They helped Irwin find workers from their prefecture. Later immigrants came mostly from surrounding prefectures.

The first groups of workers from Japan had their boat trip paid for by the plantation owners. They were promised much more pay than they would have been able to make in Japan. But when they arrived they found that they were receiving the lowest pay of all plantation workers. They found that living in Hawaii was more expensive than in Japan. Still most were able to send a little money home, and some saved money and returned to Japan after their contracts were completed. Many also

Japanese workers lived in buildings like this one in Honolulu

Library of Congress

Fred Kinzaburo Makino was born to an English silk merchant and a Japanese mother in 1877. He was sent away from Yokohama, Japan, by his brother, to Honolulu, Hawaii, to start a store. Because Makino had learned English in school, he was able to help his Japanese customers with their legal problems. Aggressive and always ready for a fight, he was a leader in the struggle for higher wages for the *Issei* plantation workers. He started a newspaper, the *Hawaii Hochi*, which is still in existence.

These workers harvested pineapples on a large Hawaiian plantation, 1925

traveled to the United States mainland in hopes of making more money.

Work on plantations was nearly unbearable and seemingly unending. Workers were not allowed to talk, and they had no chance to rest. The *lunas*, or overseers, would whip them if they slowed their pace.

Some Japanese immigrants who came to Hawaii were former soldiers

All workers—men, women, and their children—lived on the plantation. Living conditions were poor. All workers slept together in a common room where they also had to cook their food.

The *Issei* plantation workers tried to improve their conditions in many different ways. It was difficult because they had few rights under Hawaiian law. Many ran away from their plantations. This was illegal because it was in violation of their contracts. There were strikes, when the Japanese workers would refuse to work unless the owners raised their pay or improved their working conditions.

Workers continued to go to Hawaii from Japan through the early 1900s. By 1920 the Japanese population in Hawaii was 109,294 —43 percent of all people in Hawaii. They are now well into their fifth generation.

The United States captured the Hawaiian Islands in 1898, using military force. In 1900, Hawaii became an official territory, part of the United States.

THE NEXT STEP: THE WEST COAST

efore 1890, few Japanese immigrants traveled to the mainland of the United States. But between 1891 and 1924 there was a large wave of immigration, with nearly 300,000 Japanese people entering the United States. Not everyone who came to America stayed. But those who did tried to make a comfortable home in a place where most people did not welcome Asians.

Why did the Japanese come? To work. Many Hawaiian plantation workers had heard that the pay was higher on the mainland of the United States. California was growing. It had a nearly endless need for manual laborers. For a long time workers had come from China, but in 1882 a law was passed preventing any more Chinese from immigrating to the United States. Japanese workers were used to replace them.

The Japanese worked canning freshly caught fish, packing meat, logging trees, refining salt, mining, and building the railroads, but most of their work was farm labor. They followed the harvests from south to north as the seasons changed. The work was hard and the pay was low.

George Shima, whose real name was Kinji Ushijima, became known as the "Potato King." Shima started as a potato picker. Then, because he knew English, he made money by finding Issei workers for white farmers. He saved money to lease land to grow potatoes. By 1912, he was farming 10,000 acres and had a fortune worth $500,000. His children went to top American colleges. When he bought a house in Berkeley, California, neighbors protested against him because he was Japanese, but he refused to move.

This farming family worked hard to gather crops in California, 1942

UPI/Bettmann

*Like other Japanese immigrants, the owners of this grocery store
in Los Angeles around 1930 struggled with discrimination*

The Japanese *Issei* were no more welcome than the Chinese had been. In legal terms, they were called "aliens ineligible for citizenship." Unlike the many European immigrants who came to America during the same time period, the Japanese and other Asians could not become citizens. That meant they could not vote, serve in the armed forces, or expect protection from the United States government.

Many politicians and other leaders in California and other western states blamed the *Issei* for unemployment among white citizens. During the early 1900s numerous attempts were made to pass laws against the Japanese immigrants. Since the *Issei* could not become citizens, they had little power to do anything about it.

In 1913, the Alien Land Law was passed in California. This law barred Japanese from buying or selling land, although they could keep what they already owned. This was just another restriction for Japanese in the United States. They were not allowed to work at many jobs or live anywhere they wanted to. The Alien Land Law, and other laws like it, were designed to make it so

difficult for Japanese to live in the United States that they would leave. By 1924, an exclusion law prevented any immigration of Japanese unless they were diplomats, students, or merchants.

The problem of anti-Japanese feeling and laws reached its worst point during World War II, when people of Japanese descent were forced into internment camps run by the U.S. government. There they waited behind barbed wire until the war ended.

*This mother and daughter both worked
on California farms, 1937*

PICTURE BRIDES

Some women came to Hawaii and later to the United States mainland with the first groups of workers. Some even brought their young children. But there were few Japanese women compared to the number of men, especially on the mainland. Many of the Issei men were becoming middle-aged and wanted to marry before they became too old.

A few Issei men married Native American women, African American women, and Mexican women. There were laws against miscegenation, which means non-white people marrying white men and women. But there weren't any laws about non-white people marrying other non-white people.

Issei men really preferred marrying women from Japan. Some went to Japan to find a wife. But most Issei men could not afford to go back to marry. Since the trend in Japan was toward arranged marriages, there was one way that the man could marry without having to go Japan. In an arranged marriage, the bride and groom do not need to know or even meet each other before they get married.

About 67,000 women came from Japan between 1908 and 1924. Most of the wives had never met their husbands. They had been married in Japan without their husbands being there. The husbands and wives only knew each other from descriptions and from pictures they had exchanged. These marriages were known as *shashin kekkon* (shah-sheen kehk-kohn), or "picture marriages." The women were known as "picture brides."

The practice of arranged marriage made many Americans angry. They did not want Issei or Nisei (nee-say), the second generation, in the United States in the first place. These people were especially afraid of a second generation who were American citizens and could speak English fluently.

In a well-loved folk tale, Momotaro was a tiny boy born from a peach

Just as in Japan, Issei mothers told stories to their children. Many Nisei (second generation) kids grew up hearing stories like the one about Momotaro (moh-moh-tah-roh), the tiny boy who was born from a peach. He made his parents proud by killing a vicious ogre, or *oni* (oh-nee), and gave his parents the *oni's* treasure. Through this story, Issei parents passed on the ideals of honoring one's parents, and the values of responsibility and duty.

They felt they would never become true Americans because they were not white.

Many of the picture brides arrived on ships to meet their husbands for the first time at the dock. They were often much younger than the men that they had married. Often, the men would immediately take the wives to a store to buy American clothes and to take a wedding picture. Then they would go to their new homes, often far away from the cities where their boat had docked.

There was really no way to prepare these women for the life that they would lead in the United States. The support of family and friends in the village was not there. Everyone spoke an unfamiliar language. There was hard work to do in the fields and in the home. *Issei* wives tended to stay in the home, especially after their children were born. They did not have the opportunities or language skills to become part of the world outside their own community. The only good thing was that there were few mothers-in-law the wives had to please.

UPI/Bettmann Newsphotos

Picture brides arrive in San Francisco, 1920

Photos courtesy of Carolyn Takeshita

This couple exchanged photos in 1907, then were married

25

STARTING COMMUNITIES

For many Japanese, starting a farm or a small business, or fishing were the only ways to make money for themselves, not someone else. The *Issei* worker could achieve his dream if he saved enough money. He could also borrow some money from a *tanomoshi* (tah-noh-moh-shee), a credit association, where other immigrants put their money together to make loans to members.

Issei relied on each other as they had in Japan. To survive, farmers and fishermen had to help each other, especially since there were laws and prejudice working against them in the United States and Hawaii. When *Issei* started farms by renting or leasing land, other *Issei* in towns and cities would start businesses to supply them with food, farming supplies, clothes, and medicine. They also started cafés, laundries, grocery stores, and barber shops.

The new brides and the children born from the marriages made it possible to form communities at last. The *Issei*'s farms required a lot of labor, which was supplied by family members, as was the practice in Japan. If they had had to hire workers, the farms would not have made enough money to survive.

At Yamato Colony, people have been growing fruits and nuts since 1908

Kyutaro Abiko was a pioneering newspaperman and businessman. He arrived in the United States in 1885 and became fluent in English. Abiko tried to think of ways for Japan and the United States to have better relations and for *Issei* to find a better life in the United States. He started a farming colony in Livingston, California, called the Yamato (yah-mah-toh) Colony, in 1908. The farmers shared expenses and farming equipment to save money. The colony still exists today, with the original farmers' descendants still growing fruits and nuts.

Issei *began opening businesses of their own in the cities*

In 1925, 46 percent of all Japanese in the United States were employed in farm labor. When you count all of the businessmen who sold farm supplies, and wives and children who worked on farms for no pay, most people either worked in agriculture or supported those who did.

The Nisei, the second generation, helped on the farm when they became older, but they also helped in other ways. After the passage of the Alien Land Law in California, Nisei were citizens of the United States and could legally own land. Many Issei began to buy and lease land in their children's names.

Most Nisei worked in their parents' businesses or farms. In many ways they lived just like most other Americans. They attended the same schools as other children and could eventually vote, run for political office, and own land. They had all the rights of citizens. But they were often treated differently because they were not

accepted as equal by some people.

Communities in the cities became larger, and more Issei began to live in the cities, opening businesses and working at many types of jobs. Some Nisei were able to attend college. Even with college degrees, few employers would hire a Nisei because of anti-Japanese discrimination.

Another thing that fueled anti-Japanese prejudice was that Japanese businesses were growing strong, and Japan had become a major military power. Many Americans began to hate and fear Japan, and could not seem to tell the difference between the Japanese in Japan and Japanese Americans.

Wing Luke Asian Museum, Seattle

These people are pounding rice to make the special New Year's treats called mochi, 1916

27

WORLD WAR II

By the late 1930s, Japan had become a military power and wanted to take over other Asian countries. By 1941, during World War II, Japan had already invaded China, Korea, and many Pacific islands. On December 7, 1941, Japan bombed U.S. Navy ships in Pearl Harbor in Hawaii. Japan felt that the American ships at Pearl Harbor were a threat. The attack brought the United States into World War II.

It was the worst nightmare for Japanese Americans. Many *Issei* believed that the war Japan was waging in China would eventually involve the United States. They were already targets of racism. What they did not know was that the president of the United States, Franklin Delano Roosevelt, had ordered a study to see whether Japanese Americans were loyal to Japan. The study found no Japanese Americans who were disloyal to the United States.

Yet right after the bombing of Pearl Harbor, more than 2,000 *Issei* were arrested by the FBI. They had committed no crime,

U.S. *ships burn at Pearl Harbor after Japan's surprise attack, December 7, 1941*

but were suspected of being spies. What fueled this hatred? Some farmers and businessmen hoped to take the property belonging to the *Issei* and *Nisei* for themselves. Some politicians thought being

When the Japanese Americans were forced from their homes, they were told they could take only what they could carry. Only the most important things could be taken. Everything else had to be given to friends to be taken care of or sold. Possessions that were locked up for storage were often broken into and stolen by the time families returned to their homes. Many Japanese American houses and businesses were vandalized.

A *child being evacuated from Los Angeles sits with the family belongings*

anti-Japanese American was a good way to get votes. As the Japanese Americans were arrested, only a few prominent Americans spoke up for them.

At the beginning of U.S. involvement in the war, things were not going well for the United States and its allies. Japan had conquered the Philippines. There were some naval battles in which the United States suffered great losses. The American public blamed the war on the Japanese Americans among them.

Top military officials in the Army and Navy recommended to the president that all Japanese Americans be removed from the West Coast of the United States. The reason given was that, whether they were Japan-born or American-born, any Japanese American could still be loyal to Japan. These officials made the recommendation even though they had no proof of any Japanese Americans spying for Japan.

On February 19, 1942, President Franklin D. Roosevelt signed Executive Order 9066, which said that all Japanese in the military zone of the West Coast were to be put in camps. Within three months, 110,000 West Coast Japanese were taken from their homes and imprisoned in temporary centers, such as the one at the Santa Anita race track near

Marcie Pottern

In 1942, Japanese Americans who lived in the shaded area were forced to move to internment camps. The names in small letters were "assembly centers." The names in big letters were permanent internment camps.

Los Angeles. Of these Japanese American families, 64 percent were American citizens. They were later moved to 12 "relocation centers," also called internment camps, in remote locations in the United States.

UPI/Bettmann Newsphotos

Japanese Americans wait for a train that will take them from Los Angeles to an internment camp

LIFE IN THE INTERNMENT CAMPS

The relocation centers and internment camps were like mass prisons with soldiers guarding the gates and fences. Anyone who stepped outside of the barbed wire fences could be shot by the guards. Some people were killed for being outside the fences of the camps. It was impossible to escape because the camps were in isolated locations where there were few people around. It also was impossible to hide one's Japanese American features.

The camps were in areas far from cities in Nevada, Arizona, Utah, New Mexico, Idaho, Colorado, Arkansas, and California. At most of the sites, the weather was freezing cold in the winter and burning hot in the summer.

The army provided drab buildings called barracks to live in. Families were cramped together in small rooms. They hung blankets or built small walls for privacy. Life in the camps was usually dull and boring. There was no freedom—no one was allowed to leave, and few visitors could come in. Food was bland and starchy, served in an army dining room called a mess hall where the wait in line was long. Bathrooms were also usually crowded, with little privacy.

After a few months, schools were set up for kids. Hospitals and health care were organized. Most of the internees, as the people in the camps were called, were forced to work on farms growing crops like sugar beets. The pay was extremely low and the work was hard. They resented being forced to work. The internees put much more care into growing fresh food in their own gardens. English language and arts and crafts classes for adults were popular.

UPI/Bettmann Newsphotos

Meals were served in large buildings called mess halls at the internment camps

Yoshiko Uchida was 11 years old when her family was uprooted from their home in Berkeley, California, and sent to a camp in the desert near Topaz, Utah. Many years later she wrote two heartwarming and sad books about her experience. *Journey to Topaz* and *Journey Home* tell the story of how kids lived behind barbed wire and what it was like when they were allowed to leave.

Boys play touch football at an internment camp

Some *Nisei* wanted to volunteer to fight in the army. They felt that serving in the army was a way to prove their loyalty to the United States. Other *Nisei* were drafted into the military by the government. The 442nd Combat Team and the 100th Battalion were made up of 33,000 Japanese Americans from Hawaii and the mainland. These units won more medals for bravery and honor than any other units in all of American military history.

Some *Nisei* felt that it was not right to fight for the United States while their families were imprisoned just for being Japanese American. Many of the *Nisei* who decided not to fight were put in jail, and their citizenship was taken away.

By the end of the war, there were fewer people in the camps. Some were able to leave the camps to go to school or work in other parts of the United States.

Few Japanese Americans in Hawaii were put into camps. This was the case even though Hawaii had a major naval base which had been attacked by Japan. Hawaii is also much closer to Japan than the U.S. mainland. Only 900 Hawaiian Japanese Americans were sent to the mainland camps. Since one-third of the Hawaiian population was of Japanese descent, most business would have completely shut down if they had all been imprisoned.

Many Nisei *fought for the United States in World War II*

31

REBUILDING JAPANESE AMERICA

Toward the end of World War II, Japanese Americans were released from the camps. When they returned to their homes, there was little left of their former lives. All of the things that most *Issei* had built over their years in the United States were gone. Many businesses, houses, and possessions were gone. The amount of money they would have made if they had been able to live their own lives was lost. It was common for families to be separated, living in different parts of the country.

Some Japanese Americans were sent to Japan. Some went willingly, having given up on any hope of a life in the United States, but some were forced to leave. Many *Nisei* who had refused to fight in the United States Army had their citizenship

A *Japanese American family in front of their house after World War II*

taken away and were put in prison. They were forced to go to Japan after the war, even though they were not citizens of Japan and had no rights there.

Astronaut Ellison Onizuka was the first Japanese American in space

Today, many *Nisei* are prominent in science and the arts, among other areas. Ellison S. Onizuka (1946–1986) was the first Japanese American astronaut. He was mourned by the nation when he died in the *Challenger* space shuttle explosion. Patsy Takemoto Mink (b. 1927) was the first *Nisei* woman elected to the U.S. House of Representatives. And Noriyuki "Pat" Morita (b. 1932) is perhaps the most famous *Nisei* actor, for his role in *The Karate Kid*.

New American citizens taking the oath of allegiance, New Jersey, 1953

Before the war, almost all Japanese Americans had lived on the West Coast of the United States. After World War II, Japanese Americans were living on the East Coast and in the Midwest as well as on the West Coast.

Thousands of Japanese Americans returned to California, Washington, and Oregon. They found that many people did not welcome their return. Daniel Inouye, now a United States senator from Hawaii, was a 442nd Combat Team veteran. He wore his uniform after returning from the war in Europe where he had been wounded and had lost an arm. Still, a barber refused to cut his hair because he was a Japanese American.

It was still not possible for Japanese Americans to live anywhere they wanted to and there still was much job discrimination. Anger and resentment against Japan and Japanese lingered and still exist to this day.

In 1952, the *Issei* were finally allowed to become citizens of the United States. More than forty years after the war, the U.S. government agreed to pay Japanese Americans reparations, money for the wrongs done to them. The American government admitted that the imprisonment of the Japanese Americans had been illegal and wrong.

In the 1950s and 1960s, job opportunities opened for *Nisei* as the American economy grew stronger. Finally, a *Nisei* could go to college and have some hope of working as a professional. But many could still find work only as gardeners and housekeepers.

Some Japanese came to the United States after World War II. Some were farmers. Some worked for Japanese corporations. The number of immigrants was relatively small, and many Japanese only lived in the U.S. for a few years. Many Japanese women came to the United States after marrying American military men who had been stationed in Japan following the war.

SAN FRANCISCO

The first Japanese immigrants to America came to the port of San Francisco. Those students, laborers, and diplomats started the first urban Japanese American community in the United States. Los Angeles has had the largest population of Japanese Americans since the early 1900s, but San Francisco has the longest history. The early community was called *Nihonjin-machi* (nee-hohn-jeen mah-chee), or Japanese town. It was the place where the *Issei* lived and did their business.

Now Japanese Americans live throughout the city. But there still is a business district known as *Nihonmachi* (nee-hohn-mah-chee), or Japantown.

The center of Japantown is a shopping center used by Japanese Americans and the new immigrants from Japan who have come since World War II. The new immigrants are responsible for starting a popular event called *Sakura Matsuri* (sah-koo-rah mot-soo-ree), the Cherry Blossom Festival. In Japan, viewing cherry blossoms in the spring is a favorite pastime in cities. In San Francisco, though, there are few cherry blossoms to admire. Instead, the celebration is best known for its parade, an American addition to the festivities.

Many institutions in Japantown serve the Japanese American community. At the senior center, for example, *Nisei* elders gather with their neighbors for lunch. There are many *dojos* (doh-johs), or practice halls, where martial arts are taught. *Judo* (joo-doh), *aikido* (eye-kee-doh), and *kendo* (ken-doh) are all martial arts that started with the fighting techniques of the *samurai*.

Many different kinds of people practice Zen meditation today

Shunryo Suzuki (1904–1971) was a Buddhist priest who came from Japan to the Japanese American Buddhist church in San Francisco. Many non-Japanese people came to him to learn how to meditate. (Meditation is sitting quietly with the goal of calming the mind.) He founded the San Francisco Zen Center to teach a simple and direct kind of Buddhism called Zen. At the Zen Center today, any morning at dawn, Zen monks in black robes sit meditating next to people in suits ready to go to the office.

The annual Cherry Blossom Festival in San Francisco features a grand parade

The Japanese American Historical Society in San Francisco keeps records on the history of Japanese Americans. The third generation, the *Sansei* (sahn-say), are having

their own children, the *Yonsei* (yohn-say), or fourth generation. They want their history to live on.

In parks in the Japantown area, two opponents may sit and play the game of Go on a park bench. The board, covered with round black-and-white pieces, shows a game of strategy as complicated as chess. Onlookers watch to see how the game is progressing. Japanese American grocery stores throughout the city carry Japanese items, such as soy sauce and Japanese-style white rice. And the city of San Francisco has churches of all denominations with Japanese American congregations, from Buddhist to Catholic.

Beneath the Japantown trade center is a traditional Japanese bath house. Here, in separate areas for men and women, bathing is done in extremely hot water that leaves the body and mind refreshed.

Japanese restaurants throughout the city serve sushi and thick hot soba noodles. Japanese architecture appears in curved roofs, and Japanese-style gardens are scattered throughout Golden Gate Park. San Francisco is full of Japanese culture brought by Japanese Americans but enjoyed by all the residents of the city.

San Francisco's Japantown

ISAMU NOGUCHI

One of the most famous sculptors of this century, Isamu Noguchi (ee-sah-moo noh-goo-chee), was a Nisei.

Noguchi was born in Los Angeles in 1904. He came from a family of writers. His father was a well known Issei writer who wrote poetry in English. His mother was a white American poet. Isamu's father moved his family to Japan in 1906. Noguchi lived in Japan until 1917, when he was 13 years old. During World War II, he went to the Poston internment camp.

Noguchi did not always know he wanted to be an artist. In fact, as a young man he studied medicine at Columbia University. But a change of heart led him to Paris. There he discovered the work of Brancusi, a sculptor. Brancusi's abstract sculptures in stone and metal could make you think of the flight of a bird without ever showing you the bird itself. Noguchi was excited by Brancusi's work and studied with him.

Soon Noguchi began creating his own works. He often made his sculptures from wood or stone, natural materials that he shaped with gentle curves and swells. They did not usually look like people or animals, but often seemed to express feelings formed of shapes and textures.

Noguchi's sculptures express some traditional Japanese qualities. They show a love of nature and a deep appreciation for the beauty of the world. They also have a modern American feeling, because each one was an expression of the creator's thoughts

Sculptor Isamu Noguchi

Listen carefully and you will hear just a faint echo, then the sound of water running gently, so gently, over stone. The sound might be coming from a Japanese garden where water drops run through a bamboo tube onto a polished stone base. But this fountain is a sculpture by Isamu Noguchi. The hollow basin in the stone was not formed by nature but by a human hand. It is a modern sculpture, with polished sides, and it gives the feeling of the artist who made it. A fountain like this creates peace, even in the middle of a busy city.

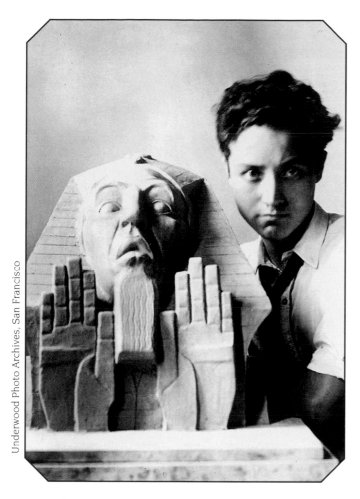

The young Noguchi with one of his sculptures

of white rice paper set over wire frames. Some are traditional lantern shapes, but others contain much wilder twists and turns. Light shining through makes his lamps look like tiny shining sculptures.

Noguchi died in 1988, known all over the world for his work. He brought peace and beauty to everything he made.

and feelings. Abstract but natural, the sculptures give the viewer a sense of peace.

The sounds of traffic barely interrupt the quiet of Noguchi's house, which is now the Noguchi Museum in Long Island City, New York. Here you can walk around the huge work space where the artist chiseled and shaped his work. His drawings hang on the walls, some done in brush and ink in the traditional Japanese style but with modern touches. The garden outside the house contains many sculptures sitting off the gravel paths and open to the elements of sun and snow.

Noguchi was a creative artist who liked to try his hand at many things. Among his best-known work are some of his simplest: lamp shades. He designed beautiful lamps

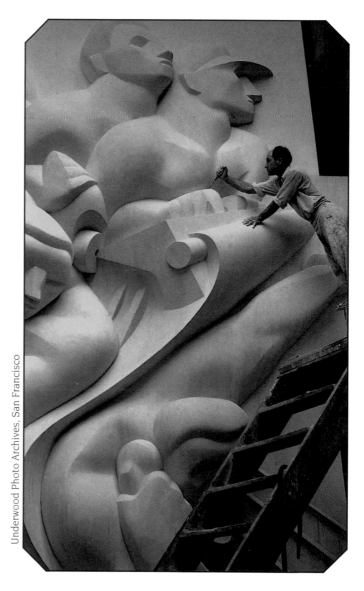

Noguchi at work

CONTEMPORARY FACES

Today, Japanese Americans are influential in many fields. Here are the stories of how four different people succeeded in the arts, sports, and politics.

U.S. *Congressman Norman Mineta with students at UCLA, 1988*

Norman Mineta (b. 1931)

Norman Mineta was born in San Jose, California. He and his family were sent to an internment camp, but he continued on the path of education and graduated from the University of California at Berkeley. After serving in the army, he became a member of San Jose's Human Relations Commission and its City Council. In 1972 he was elected mayor of San Jose. Norman Mineta was the first Japanese American to be the mayor of a major city in the United States outside of Hawaii. He is now a United States Congressman representing his district in San Jose.

Jeanne Wakatsuki Houston (b. 1934)

Jeanne Wakatsuki Houston overcame suffering to make something beautiful. When she was only eight years old, she and her family were forced to move to the internment camp at Manzanar, California. She felt she must have committed some crime to suffer so much.

Thirty years later, Houston was able to write about her experiences in her best-selling book, *Farewell to Manzanar*, which tells the story of what her family went through. Her husband, James D. Houston, was her co-author on the book and also on a prize-winning film of the same name. Today she is at work on a book about the picture brides who came to America to marry Japanese men and the role of Japanese women in settling the American West.

Jeanne Wakatsuki was sent to an internment camp with her parents

Christian Steiner

Conductor Seiji Ozawa

Kristi Yamaguchi (b. 1971)

Kristi Yamaguchi's grace on the ice makes skating look easy, but she practiced for thousands of hours before winning an Olympic gold medal. Like Seiji Ozawa, she had to overcome a handicap to perform. She was born with feet that curved in and down, which had to be corrected by wearing special shoes. She began to skate when she was five, often getting up before dawn to practice. In 1992, Yamaguchi became the first Japanese American woman to win an Olympic gold medal for ice skating. As a *Yonsei*, or fourth-generation Japanese American, she serves as an inspiration for all American kids.

Seiji Ozawa (b. 1935)

Music fueled the life of Seiji Ozawa. As a child in Japan, he wanted to become a pianist. But when he was 16 his hands were injured and he could no longer play. Instead of giving up, he decided to study to become a conductor.

After coming to the United States, Ozawa started conducting at the Berkshire Music Festival and went on to lead many famous orchestras, including the San Francisco Symphony. He is now musical director of the Boston Symphony Orchestra. This Japanese American conductor is famous for his energetic style as he stands in front of hundreds of musicians. Watching him, you can feel as well as hear the music as it begins to swell.

Reuters/Bettmann

Figure skater Kristi Yamaguchi won a Gold Medal in the 1992 Olympic Games

JAPANESE AMERICAN LIFE TODAY

If you are a Japanese American child today, your life is probably not that much different from your non-Japanese American friends. It's likely that one of your parents is Japanese and one not, so you may have European origins as well. Today, at least half of Japanese Americans get married outside of their ethnic group, usually to European Americans.

Japanese Americans are most likely to live around cities on the West Coast or Hawaii. They are in all types of employment—in professions, blue-collar work, and the arts. They are no longer forced to live around Japantowns in the central areas of cities.

There are other changes, too. The *Issei* generation is almost all gone. *Nisei* are mostly senior citizens. Most *Nisei* and *Sansei* grew up in nuclear families, with just a mother, father, and children. *Sansei* and *Yonsei* are raised much more like American children than like Japanese children.

Many *Nisei*, *Sansei* and *Yonsei* attend Japanese American churches which serve as social centers. They often join Japanese American athletic leagues. Most *Sansei* are of the baby-boom generation, which means they were born between 1946 and 1960. They are much more American than Japanese, but they still have their Japanese side.

For many Japanese American families, *Oshogatsu* is still the most important event of the year. They might make *mochi* together, a type of cake made from pounding rice.

Sports such as baseball are popular among Japanese Americans

One way that Japanese Americans like to get together is by participating in sports. *Nisei* started many sports leagues which are still active from California to Washington State. *Sansei* and *Yonsei* are carrying on the tradition. Sports leagues are not just for fun and recreation. They also allow Japanese Americans to socialize with each other. In many cities, the Japantowns used to be places where Japanese Americans lived and worked. Now Japanese Americans live all over, so sports is one of the few ways left to keep the community alive.

Chris Tucker

Japanese American families share closeness across the generations

Many families dance in the *Obon* festivities every summer. When a relative dies, they often observe the funeral with a Buddhist ceremony.

In Hawaii, Japanese Americans, particularly the *Sansei*, see themselves as part of the local culture—part Japanese, part Hawaiian, part American. They feel comfortable in this mix of races and cultures.

One thing that has not changed is respect for one's parents. In the Japanese American family, aging grandparents are taken care of at home as much as possible, rather than being moved into nursing homes.

Most Japanese now come to the United States to work for Japanese corporations. They typically stay for a few years and then return to Japan. Japanese American children of recent immigrants are likely to attend a Japanese language school on weekends. All subjects are taught in Japanese, to prepare the students for their possible return to Japan.

Some Japanese Americans still have strong ties to Japan. But many Japanese Americans no longer feel any ties to Japan at all. As time goes on, there may be little to distinguish Japanese Americans from other Americans. But the history and contributions of Japanese Americans to the culture of the United States will live on.

Photo courtesy of Tozai Times

Girls wear traditional clothing in a Nisei Week parade

CONTRIBUTIONS TO AMERICAN CULTURE

Japanese Americans make up less than 1 percent of the population of the United States, but they have had a strong influence on many areas of American culture. From large farms to beautiful gardens, the hard work and talent of Japanese Americans have enriched the lives of many Americans.

The word for the United States in Japanese was *Beikoku* (bay-koh-koo), meaning rice country. Rice was the symbol of wealth, so it meant that the United States was a country of wealth and plenty. It is also appropriate because *Issei* farmers had such a large role in the development of agriculture and the fishing industry on the West Coast.

Japanese immigrants started farms on dry, rocky land that most people thought was useless for farming. Through hard work they cleared and planted fields and brought water to dry areas with irrigation.

Japanese Americans practice the traditional art of taiko drumming

They were able to take land that no one wanted and make it productive. In this way, Japanese farmers helped California become the agricultural giant of the West Coast.

Truck farming, the selling of fruits and vegetables by the farmers themselves, was started by *Issei* farmers. Before World War II, many Japanese farmers close to cities

---

As busy as the *Issei* were, whether they lived in the city or the country, they found time to express themselves in art. Japanese people love music, paintings, and other forms of art. *Issei* started clubs of all sorts to learn and develop their singing, dancing, and other creative talents.

It is in the fine arts and literature that many *Issei* made their largest contributions. *Haiku* (high-koo) is a short poetic form—just three lines and 17 syllables—that was very popular among the *Issei*. In Japan, *haiku* uses images from nature and the seasons. Many *Issei* belonged to poetry clubs and wrote about their everyday lives, rather than about nature.

Japanese painting, which uses special brushes and strokes, is another contribution the Japanese brought with them to America. Chiura Obata (1885–1975) was a professor at the University of California, Berkeley, from 1932 to 1954. He introduced many Americans to *sumi-e* (soo-mee-eh), the art of brush painting.

Sushi is a popular dish in restaurants today

topped with seaweed and different types of vegetables and fish.

Sake (sah-keh) means liquor in Japanese, but is the name for a special liquor made from rice. Today there are *sake* distilleries in the United States, all using American-grown rice. Since American *sake* cannot be sold in Japan, almost all of the *sake* made in the United States is consumed here.

Japanese fisherman since the early 1900s caught tuna, salmon, octopus, and abalone. They made popular many types of fish that were not eaten before in the United States.

Some Japanese vegetables became widely eaten after Japanese farmers began to cultivate them. *Napa* (nah-pah), a kind of cabbage, *daikon* (dye-kohn), a kind of radish, and *mikan* (mih-kan), tangerines, can now all can be found in large grocery stores.

Mushrooms had been growing in the mountains of the West Coast before there were people living in North America. When *Issei* arrived in America, they discovered varieties of mushrooms, or *matsutake*

found that the best way to sell their fruits and vegetables was to drive them to market for sale. They first started selling to other Japanese American retailers, then began selling directly to customers as well. This way, they were able to sell their produce fresher and at lower prices.

It is no surprise that one of the biggest contributions by Japanese Americans was to cultivate Japanese rice. California proved to have very good rice-growing conditions. Japanese-style rice has a shorter grain than rice that is grown in many other Asian countries. It is also stickier. Many non-Japanese Americans have grown to love Japanese rice.

Rice can be eaten by itself or used as an ingredient in other dishes. *Sushi* (soo-shee) is one Japanese rice dish that has become popular in the United States. To make *sushi*, rice is seasoned, mixed with many ingredients, and shaped, rolled, or

San Francisco Convention & Visitors Bureau

The flower industry owes much to the hard work of Japanese Americans

43

Today, Japanese Americans work in every field

(mah-tsoo-tah-keh), that they remembered from Japan. They went on trips to the mountains to pick them every autumn. *Nisei* later carried on the practice. Different varieties of Japanese *matsutake* can be bought in many gourmet produce markets all over the United States.

Japanese Americans have also been successful at growing flowers and other plants for decorative gardens. If you live in the San Francisco Bay Area or around Los Angeles, the flowers decorating your table may have been grown by Japanese American flower growers. They were some of the earliest flower growers in California. Since it was possible to grow flowers on small plots of land near cities, *Issei* flower growers could transport their flowers easily to market. Now most flowers are grown in large greenhouses. Everyone loves flowers, so it has been a successful industry for many Japanese Americans.

Starting in the early 1900s, many Japanese plants became popular in gardens all over the United States. The Japanese

Tea Garden in Golden Gate Park in San Francisco was designed by Makoto Hagiwara in the late 1800s. It became known across the country.

Around that time, demand for imported plants began to grow. In San Francisco, the Domoto Brothers, Kanetaro and Takanoshin, began to import many Japanese varieties from Japan to California: camellias, Japanese maple, ginko, azaleas, cryptomerias, wisteria, loquat, Japanese chestnut, and persimmons.

Now, Japanese plants are common in the United States. Cherry blossom trees bloom in Washington, D.C. in the spring. Wisterias are a common sight in the southern United States.

Issei were restricted in their work, so many started their own farms. Many others started small businesses that served the needs of farmers. Many *Nisei* and *Sansei* have carried on their work up to the present. Japanese Americans have forever changed the American landscape and the eating habits of all Americans.

44

INDEX

Other books about Japanese Americans:

Japanese American Curriculum Project. *Japanese American Journey: The Story of a People*. JACP, Inc., 1985.

Hamanaka, Sheila. *The Journey: Japanese-Americans, Racism, and Renewal*. Orchard Books, 1990.

Kitano, Harry. *Japanese Americans*. Chelsea House, 1993.

Moynihan, Daniel P., ed. *Japanese Americans* (The Peoples of North American Series). Knowledge Unlimited, 1994.

Westridge Young Writers Workshop. *Kids Explore America's Japanese American Heritage*. Santa Fe, N.M.: John Muir Publications, 1994.

EXTREMELY WEIRD SERIES

All of the titles are written by Sarah Lovett, 8½" x 11", 48 pages, $9.95 paperback, $14.95 hardcover, with color photographs and illustrations.

Extremely Weird Bats
Extremely Weird Birds
Extremely Weird Endangered Species
Extremely Weird Fishes
Extremely Weird Frogs
Extremely Weird Insects
Extremely Weird Mammals
Extremely Weird Micro Monsters
Extremely Weird Primates
Extremely Weird Reptiles
Extremely Weird Sea Creatures
Extremely Weird Snakes
Extremely Weird Spiders

X-RAY VISION SERIES

Each title in the series is 8½" x 11", 48 pages, $9.95 paperback, with color photographs and illustrations, and written by Ron Schultz.

Looking Inside the Brain
Looking Inside Cartoon Animation
Looking Inside Caves and Caverns
Looking Inside Sports Aerodynamics
Looking Inside Sunken Treasure
Looking Inside Telescopes and the Night Sky

THE KIDDING AROUND TRAVEL GUIDES

All of the titles listed below are 64 pages and $9.95 paperbacks, except for *Kidding Around the National Parks* and *Kidding Around Spain*, which are 108 pages and $12.95 paperbacks.

Kidding Around Atlanta
Kidding Around Boston, 2nd ed.
Kidding Around Chicago, 2nd ed.
Kidding Around the Hawaiian Islands
Kidding Around London
Kidding Around Los Angeles
Kidding Around the National Parks
  of the Southwest
Kidding Around New York City, 2nd ed.
Kidding Around Paris
Kidding Around Philadelphia
Kidding Around San Diego
Kidding Around San Francisco
Kidding Around Santa Fe
Kidding Around Seattle
Kidding Around Spain
Kidding Around Washington, D.C., 2nd ed.

MASTERS OF MOTION SERIES

Each title in the series is 10¼" x 9", 48 pages, $9.95 paperback, with color photographs and illustrations.

How to Drive an Indy Race Car
  David Rubel
How to Fly a 747
  Tim Paulson
How to Fly the Space Shuttle
  Russell Shorto

THE KIDS EXPLORE SERIES

Each title is written by kids for kids by the Westridge Young Writers Workshop, 7" x 9", and $9.95 paperback, with photographs and illustrations by the kids.

Kids Explore America's Hispanic Heritage 112 pages
Kids Explore America's African American Heritage 128 pages
Kids Explore the Gifts of Children with Special Needs 128 pages
Kids Explore America's Japanese American Heritage 144 pages

ENVIRONMENTAL TITLES

Habitats: *Where the Wild Things Live*
Randi Hacker and Jackie Kaufman
8½" x 11", 48 pages, color illustrations, $9.95 paper

The Indian Way: *Learning to Communicate with Mother Earth*
Gary McLain
7" x 9", 114 pages, two-color illustrations, $9.95 paper

Rads, Ergs, and Cheeseburgers: *The Kids' Guide to Energy and the Environment*
Bill Yanda
7" x 9", 108 pages, two-color illustrations, $13.95 paper

The Kids' Environment Book: *What's Awry and Why*
Anne Pedersen
7" x 9", 192 pages, two-color illustrations, $13.95 paper

BIZARRE & BEAUTIFUL SERIES

A spirited and fun investigation of the mysteries of the five senses in the animal kingdom.

Each title in the series is 8½" x 11", $9.95 paperback, $14.95 hardcover, with color photographs and illustrations throughout.

Bizarre & Beautiful Ears
Bizarre & Beautiful Eyes
Bizarre & Beautiful Feelers
Bizarre & Beautiful Noses
Bizarre & Beautiful Tongues

RAINBOW WARRIOR SERIES

What is a Rainbow Warrior Artist? It is a person who strives to live in harmony with the Earth and all living creatures, and who tries to better the world while living his or her life in a creative way.

Each title is written by Reavis Moore with a foreword by LeVar Burton, and is 8½" x 11", 48 pages, $14.95 hardcover, with color photographs and illustrations.

Native Artists of Africa
Native Artists of North America
Native Artists of Europe

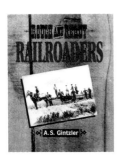

ROUGH AND READY SERIES

Learn about the men and women who settled the American West. Explore the myths and legends about these courageous individuals and learn about the environmental, cultural, and economic legacies they left to us.

Each title in the series is written by A. S. Gintzler and is 48 pages, 8½" x 11", $12.95 hardcover, with two-color illustrations and duotone archival photographs.

Rough and Ready Cowboys
Rough and Ready Homesteaders
Rough and Ready Loggers

Rough and Ready
 Outlaws & Lawmen
Rough and Ready Prospectors
Rough and Ready Railroaders

AMERICAN ORIGINS SERIES

Many of us are the third and fourth generation of our families to live in America. Learn what our great-great-grandparents experienced when they arrived here and how much of our lives are still intertwined with theirs.

Each title is 48 pages, 8½" x 11", $12.95 hardcover, with two-color illustrations and duotone archival photographs.

Tracing Our English Roots
Tracing Our French Roots
Tracing Our German Roots
Tracing Our Irish Roots

Tracing Our Italian Roots
Tracing Our Japanese Roots
Tracing Our Jewish Roots
Tracing Our Polish Roots